Trampolining

Written in association with
British Gymnastics

Produced for A & C Black by

Monkey Puzzle Media Ltd
Little Manor Farm, The Street
Brundish, Woodbridge
Suffolk IP13 8BL

Published in 2009 by

A & C Black Publishers Ltd
36 Soho Square, London W1D 3QY
www.acblack.com

First edition 2009

Copyright © 2009
British Gymnastics

ISBN: 978 0 7136 8941 9

A CIP record for this book is available from the
British Library.

Note: While every effort has been made to ensure
that the content of this book is as technically accurate
and as sound as possible, neither the author nor the
publisher can accept responsibility for any injury or
loss sustained as a result of the use of this material.

This book is produced using paper that is made
from wood grown in managed, sustainable forests.
It is natural, renewable and recyclable. The logging
and manufacturing processes conform to the
environmental regulations of the country of origin.

Acknowledgements
Cover and inside design by James Winrow and
Tom Morris for Monkey Puzzle Media Ltd.
Cover photograph courtesy of Getty Images.
The publishers would like to thank the following
for permission to use photographs: Sue Freeman
pages 4–5, 6 (top), 7, 10–11, 18–19, 20, 39, 40,
43 (top, bottom), 47, 49, 52–53 and PA Photos
pages 6 (bottom), 9, 25, 43 (middle), 45, 48.
All illustrations by Dave Saunders, except pages 7
and 44 by Jeff Edwards.

The publishers would like to thank Sue Freeman for
all her hard work as the author and consultant and
Doreen Jones for proofreading.

KNOW THE GAME is a registered trademark.

Printed and bound in China by C&C Offset
Printing Co., Ltd

CONTENTS

INTRODUCTION

Competitive trampolining is a judged action sport, like diving, symbolising freedom, flying and grace, as well as boldness and precision. Whether you are a complete beginner, an interested parent, a regular bouncer or haven't bounced for some time, this book explains the rules, equipment and skills of trampolining, as well as guiding you through the key techniques, moves and technology.

A YOUNG SPORT

Modern trampolining emerged from the prototype apparatus built by George Nissen and Larry Griswold, USA, in Nissen's garage in 1936. The first trampoline was a piece of canvas attached to an iron frame using springs. Nissen called his invention a trampoline after the Spanish word for diving board, *el trampolin*. By the early 1960s, trampolining was a competitive sport.

Modern trampolines are capable of projecting an athlete to such a height that the top stars can touch 10m high ceilings and perform repeated triple somersaults.

FÉDÉRATION INTERNATIONALE DE GYMNASTIQUE (FIG)

FIG is the organising body for international gymnastics competitions, including those included in the Olympic Games. FIG sets the international rules and determines how competitions are run.

 The parts of a trampoline.

Frame mats covering springs

Centre cross

Box

Floor mat

End deck | Bed | Metal frame

Multi-trampoline set ups have beds end to end, or side to side.

TRAINING HALL

The height of the training hall should be at least 5m for recreational use and a minimum of 8m for national and international competitions. For safety purposes, floor mats should be placed around each trampoline.

Trampoline facilities vary considerably, from those that are full time dedicated trampoline centres to those in which equipment has to be frequently erected, dismantled and stored.

TRAMPOLINE

There are a variety of sizes and types of beds suspended from metal frames by strong steel springs or cables. The beds are made from woven nylon mesh, usually marked with a red cross in the centre and an inner rectangle to define the bounce area.

Trampoline frames are either freestanding or installed over a pit in the floor. Frame pads cover the springs and the edge of the frame. Thick foam mats supported on strong metal frames, called end decks, can be attached to the ends of the trampoline. The space under and around each trampoline should be matted and clear.

End decks attached to each end of the trampoline provide an extended safe landing zone.

CLOTHING

No specialist clothing is needed, but beginners are advised to wear long-sleeved tops and tracksuit bottoms to protect their elbows and knees. Generally, clothing should be comfortable, loose or stretchable to allow movement, with no buttons, zips or buckles. Socks or trampoline shoes should be worn to prevent toes from going through the webbing. Hair must be tied back and nails kept short. All jewellery must be removed.

PUSH-IN MATS

Push-in mats are also referred to as spotter mats and are used on the bed or pushed in under the descending trampolinist to prevent bad landings that may lead to injury. In training, mats may be used for initial attempts at back and front landings.

The person sliding in the push-in mat, both in training and competition, must be trained, experienced and familiar with the performer.

For safety purposes, push-in mats are allowed at competitions (China's Huang Shanshan falls during her routine at the Beijing 2008 Olympics, China).

JUDO BELT

A soft, strong fabric belt, called a judo belt, is useful for supporting single somersaults. The belt is wrapped around the waist of the performer and the coach initially stands on the bed and can allow an increasing amount of slack as the performer progresses.

Casual, loose clothes may be worn for training, but they must not be able to 'flap'.

OVERHEAD RIG

The overhead rig is a valuable training aid to build confidence safely when complicated moves are first taught. A harness connected to a rope and pulley system may be used for learning somersaults.

The trampolinist wears the harness around the waist while a qualified coach uses the rope to control the descent of the performer. The person supervising the use of the rig must be suitably qualified and be able to control the descent of the pupil.

The coach checks the equipment every session, but it is recommended that it is also inspected annually by a specialist.

Trampolining should always be supervised by a qualified British Gymnastics coach who is responsible for assessing the suitability of the environment.

 To ensure the overhead rig is safe check:
1. the position of the trampoline under the centre of the rig
2. the security of the ropes, their attachments, and the condition of elastics and attachments on bungee rigs
3. that the swivels and pulleys have free movement
4. the belt's security
5. the ability of the supporter to hold the weight and control the descent of the pupil
6. that the coach, pupil and person controlling the push-in mat all understand their roles and are ready.

SAFETY

Trampolining is a potentially dangerous sport and the British Gymnastics Code of Practice describes what British Gymnastics recommends as the best and safest coaching practice.

BASIC SAFETY RULES

Trampolining can be safe and fun if you follow some basic rules.

- A coach must be present whenever a trampoline is in use.
- The coach must be made aware of any medical condition, injuries or medication that might affect the trampolinist's performance.
- A trained person must supervise the unfolding and folding of the trampoline.
- Never swing on or go under the trampoline, end decks or mats.
- Trampolining shoes or socks must always be worn.
- First turns must include a warm-up to minimise the risk of strained or pulled muscles.
- Never attempt a new skill without progressive training and the permission of the coach.
- Keep turns short (1–1½ minutes) – tiredness leads to poor concentration.
- Go at your own pace and don't try to copy others who may be far more capable.

- Spotters should pay attention to the person on the trampoline.
- Always listen to your coach.
- Never eat or drink around the trampolining area.
- Ensure there are sufficient spotters before getting on to the trampoline.
- When leaving the bed, walk to the edge and stop, sit or stand on the frame before getting down facing the trampoline.
- Only one person should bounce on a bed at a time.
- No projectiles or flying objects should be used in the same room.

LOOKING FOR A CLUB

British Gymnastics' core criteria enables clubs to work towards nationally recognised accreditation. GymMark, the accreditation scheme, recognises a quality club as 'safe, effective and child-friendly'. See the BG website for all GymMark clubs.

The full British Gymnastics Code of Practice can be found on www.british-gymnastics.org.

COACHING

British Gymnastics (BG) promotes current best coaching practice through its education programme, and also provides codes of practice and ethics. Before someone becomes a trampolining coach they should attend a BG coaching course and pass examinations.

COACHING QUALIFICATIONS

In trampolining, there are six levels of qualification:

- Level 0 Proficiency Award Coach
- Level 1 Assistant Coach
- Level 2 Coach
- Level 3 Club Coach
- Level 4 Senior Coach
- Level 5 High Performance Coach.

There are no entry requirements (other than being over 16 years old) to become a Level 1 Assistant Coach. To progress, the potential coach must pass each level of qualification in sequence.

MOVE PROGRESSIONS

Trampolining is potentially a dangerous sport so skills are learned gradually, by going through a series of safe progressions. Each part of a skill must be performed consistently and correctly by the trampolinist before advancing.

Long Term Athlete Development (LTAD) is especially relevant to trampolining as a sport, as many competitors participate at the highest levels well into their thirties. This means that it could take 10 years or more for a competitor to reach their full potential.

The basic moves (see pages 18–25) form the foundation for learning more advanced skills. When the less complex skills are learned gradually, progression on to more challenging skills can be done safely and accurately.

 Open and clear communication are key skills in a trampolining coach.

BRITISH GYMNASTICS TRAMPOLINE PROFICIENCY SCHEME

The proficiency scheme is a series of awards that has been devised to motivate individuals and provide a safe learning pathway. Each award consists of individual or simple combinations of moves and a sequence of skills in a routine.

- Awards 1 to 5: for the very young (under five years old) and those with disabilities.
- Awards 6 to 10: for normal school children and adults.
- Awards 11 to 15: for the more advanced performer.

BRITISH GYMNASTICS COMPETITIONS

The National Grading System of competitions (see page 40) is closely linked with safe move progressions where realistic and attainable targets for improvement are set at every level. Success is rewarded by advancement through the levels.

LOG BOOKS

British Gymnastics recommends the use of log books to measure, monitor and record individual progress. Most clubs keep records logging their members' development. They can be a great motivator when used regularly.

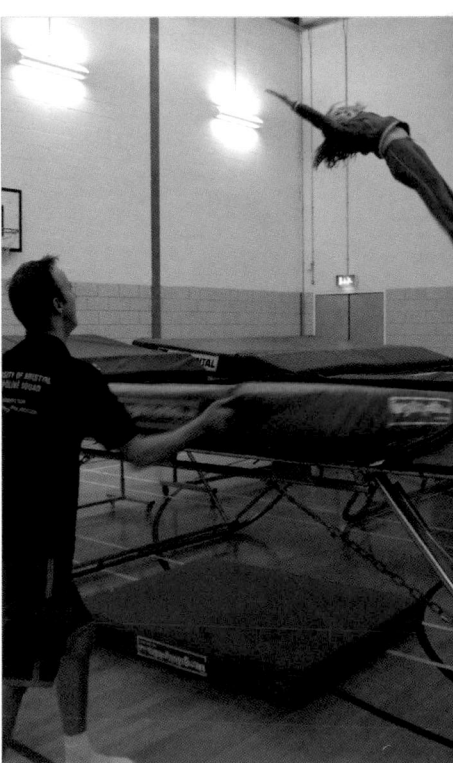

◀ More advanced performers may qualify to compete at the highest levels.

▶ Coaches are essential at every level as they impose the discipline required to be able to bounce safely and correctly.

THE CORE SKILLS

Trampolining involves jumping up and down and going from one landing to another with a rotation, twist or both in one of the allowed shapes in the flight phase. A competitive routine comprises ten different jump skills, with only one bed contact between each. Competitive trampolining is about performing these elements accurately – balancing the height of each move with the rotation and twist required.

BASIC ELEMENTS

All trampolining moves have three basic elements:

1. take-off from maximum depression of the bed to last contact

2. flight (the skill phase) from last contact to first contact

3. landing from first contact to maximum depression.

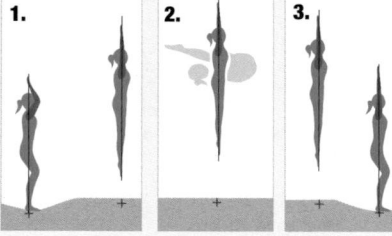

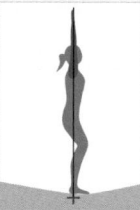

The neutral position should be shown, even briefly, on every foot landing.

THE NEUTRAL POSITION

This is a theoretical ideal position shown at the maximum depression of the bed on foot landings, where the body has finished compensating for any rotary movement from the previous move, but before preparation for any required twist or somersault rotation in the next. In reality it is sometimes necessary to prepare slightly early for a following move, so the neutral position has to be adapted. The ideal neutral position is as follows:

• body upright

• sighting forward

• legs bent ready to push.

THE TAKE-OFF PHASE

This is concerned with developing height and rotation in preparation for the flight phase by harnessing the recoil from the bed. Take-off starts at the maximum depression and continues until the last contact with the bed. The vertical force created by the recoil of the bed, position of the body and the muscular extension of the knees, ankles and feet provides the necessary force to gain enough height, twist or somersault to complete the move in the flight phase.

Take-offs from feet fall into five types (see right).

NON-FOOT TAKE-OFFS

Some moves do not land on the feet (see pages 20–23) so the subsequent take-off has to be from that position. Non-foot take-offs fall into three categories in competition (see right).

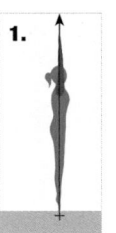
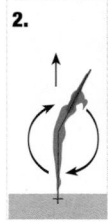
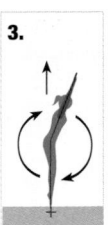
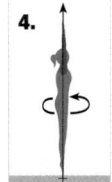

1. Straight jump
2. Back somersault rotation
3. Forward somersault rotation
4. Twist
5. Twist and somersault
6. From seat
7. From back
8. From front

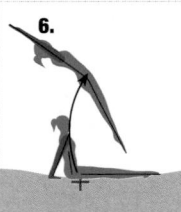
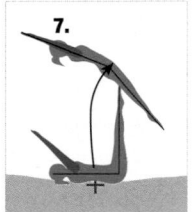

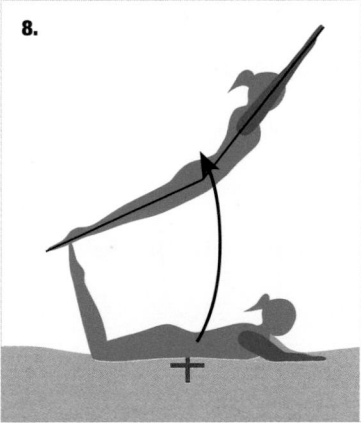

The angles and forces created on last contact with the bed determine how much rotation is possible and cannot be changed in the air.

THE FLIGHT PHASE

The flight phase starts immediately after the last contact with the bed and ends with first contact. This is where shaping, speeding up or slowing down twist and rotation take place.

In routines the gymnast is expected to use the full elasticity of the bed by doing a continuous arm swing through neutral, and fully extending their legs and toes at the beginning of the flight before performing the shape, somersault or twist.

SHAPE

There are three basic shapes: straight, tucked and piked.

A pike straddle is a variation of a pike shape and is only used in jumps, never in somersaults or twists.

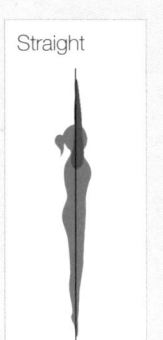

Straight

Tuck

Pike

ROTATION

There are two types of rotation – somersault and twist.

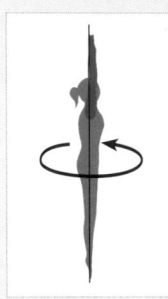

Above: Somersault rotation ('head over heels' rotating around the somersault axis). This is easiest in a tuck position, as short objects somersault more easily.
Above right: Twist rotation (turning to face another way rotating around the twist axis). This is easiest in the straight position, as narrow objects spin more easily.

PREPARATION FOR LANDING

Checking the position of the bed or end frame is vital towards the end of any move so the gymnast can accurately prepare for landing.

LINE OUT

As the competitor becomes more competent a straight, non-twisting line (line out) can be introduced on exit from somersaults and held from the shape to the landing. Eventually the line out should be shown from the upside-down vertical position through to at least a quarter past before the line is broken in preparation to land.

THE ARM SWING

Arm swing is used to generate upwards movement, and to assist balance in straight jumps. The arm lift should happen as a consequence of the bed being driven down with the legs, allowing the body to be brought upright.

Before taking off for skills, the arms need to be above the head at the maximum depression of the bed. Beginners can leave their arms up between moves, but need to learn the arm set for when they become stable at height.

BEGINNERS AND ARM SWING

Beginners do not need height, they need stability, and so it is not essential to learn the arm swing early. Arm swing can be introduced when height is necessary for progression. There are many variations of arm swing so those illustrated are just typical examples

 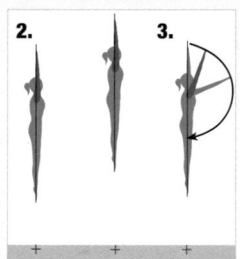 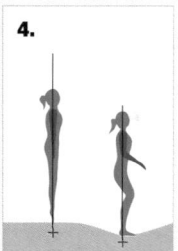

Straight jumping for height
1. Take-off. Arms swing up to the front and top.
2. Flight. Arms vertical just after leaving the bed.
3. Arms remain straight and up until just before the landing, then swing straight down the sides.

4. Landing. Arms remain down until neutral position.

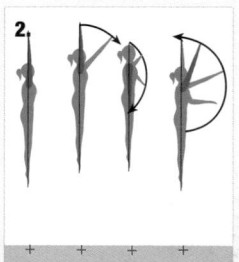 

Arm set for starting a routine
1. Take-off. Arms swing up the front to the top.
2. Flight. Arms are brought down to the sides then immediatley swung back up.
3. Landing. Arms up ready to take off for the first skill.

THE LANDING PHASE

This is where contact with the bed takes place to control any twist or rotation from the last move. On foot landings, the aim is to return to the neutral position in preparation for the next move.

Landing is the process that starts as the feet, or other parts of the body, touch the bed and continues on to the maximum depression. The aim is to have the body in the correct position to start the set up for the next move by the time maximum depression is reached. As well as the foot landing there are three other landing positions allowed in competitions – seat landing, back landing and front landing (see pages 21–23).

Hands and knees and flat back landings are used only when learning new moves.

All trampolining moves should be performed on the centre cross. The illustrations in this book are sequential, for clarity, so the performance appears to move left to right. In reality all moves should take-off and land in the same place.

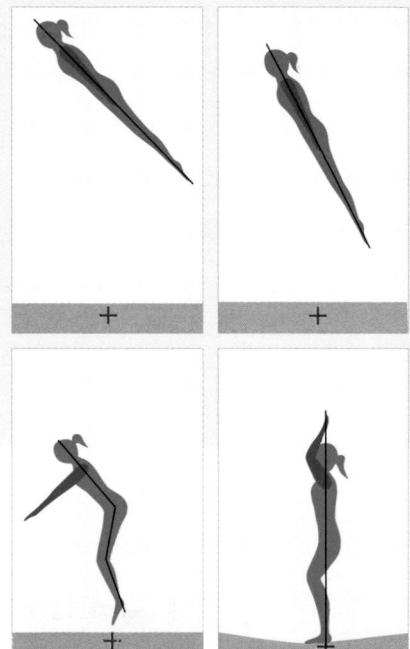

The landing phase.

LINKING SKILLS AND ROUTINES

Trampoline competition is about performing skills consecutively without straight bounces in between. This is known as a routine. Linking one skill with another is one of the most important single aspects of trampolining, as it is what differentiates the sport from the otherwise similar sport of diving. Trampoline competitions are based on routines where the competitor has to complete ten different skills after a few introductory straight jumps with only one bed contact between each.

Each level of the British Gymnastics proficiency scheme has routines for learning. All the routines give a good indication of what skills and combinations are suitable for a given level of performer.

> **All trampoline moves should be performed on the centre cross.**

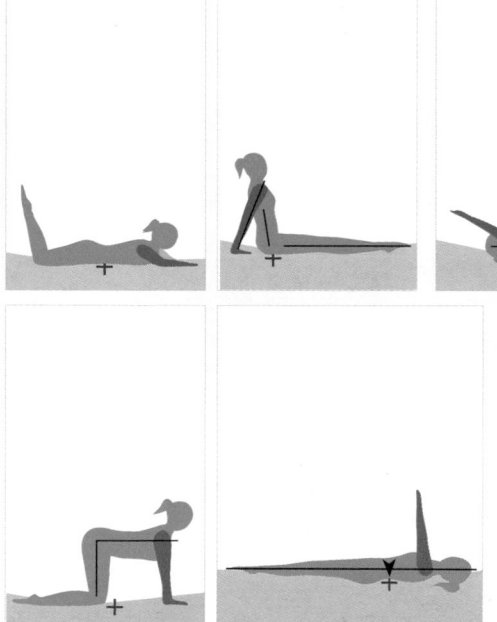

As well as the foot landing there are three other landing positions allowed in competitions – seat landing, back landing and front landing (also see pages 21–23).

Hands and knees and flat back landings are used only when learning new moves and not in competitions.

THE BASIC MOVES

Trampolining is a sport of consequences: if the basic moves are not learned correctly the competitor has little chance of being able to perform the advanced skills safely and accurately.

STOPPING

It is important for safety to learn to balance and control the bed right from the start. One of the first actions a beginner has to learn is how to kill the bounce. This means deliberately stopping the bed from moving by using a deep knee bend as the feet make contact with it.

STRAIGHT JUMP

Straight jumping creates height to give time for the skills to be accurately performed. Trampolinists should not attempt this before they have learned to control the trampoline. Teenagers easily attain uncontrolled height and risk serious injury. Most basic skills can be learned from 'press and go' or three very small bounces with no arm swing.

STRAIGHT SHAPE

To perform the straight shape:

• head, body, and legs should be in a straight line without any bend

• keep toes and feet pointed.

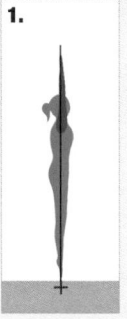 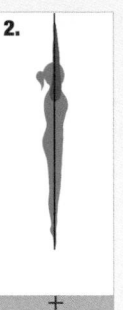 

Straight jump
1. Take-off last contact
2. Flight
3. Landing

Straight jumping is bouncing on the cross to gain height, with no somersault or twist rotation.

> **The word 'jump' is used for non-somersaulting moves that both take off and land on the feet.**

SHAPED JUMPS

Shaped jumps take off like a straight jump, then move quickly into the shape towards the top of the move, coming fast out of the shape to show a straight line before landing. The shapes described here are identical to those required in somersaulting moves and are important to get right from the start. Beginners should not attempt an arm swing with these moves but should first learn them with either press and go, or with low bounces with arms already up.

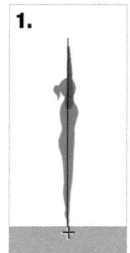  

Tuck jump
1. Take-off last contact
2. Flight
3. Landing approach

TUCK JUMP

To perform the tuck shape:

- keep legs together, fully bent at the hips and knees
- the ankles, feet and toes should be pointed
- hands must grasp the shins.

The shin grip is particularly important as it is expected by the Execution Judges in competitions and is also necessary when performing somersaults.

The tuck shape is arguably the easiest to learn but the hardest to perfect.

PIKE JUMP

To perform the pike shape:

- keep feet and legs together
- keep feet and toes pointed
- legs should be straight
- bend deeply at the hips
- extend hands towards feet.

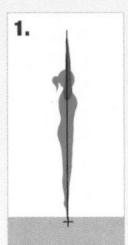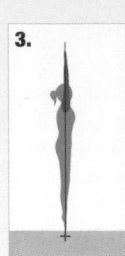

Piked jump
1. Take-off last contact
2. Flight
3. Landing

PIKED STRADDLE JUMP

The piked straddle is not considered a different shape to pike, however the legs are kept wider apart than the shoulders and ideally at an angle greater than 90 degrees. It is never allowed in somersaults.

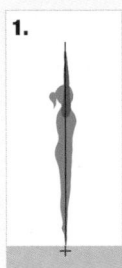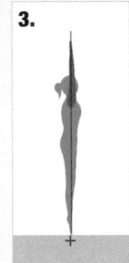

Piked straddle shape
1. Take-off last contact
2. Flight top of bounce
3. Landing

To gain the fully doubled shape without risk of pulled muscles requires a planned warm-up and stretching exercises.

 A trampolinist practises the piked straddle jump.

NON-FOOT LANDINGS

The take-offs for non-foot landings are similar to a straight jump, but with varying amounts of somersault rotation set up on last contact. More advanced versions of these landings include the pike or tuck shape in the flight phase of the move.

SEAT LANDING

1. Take off with a small amount of backward rotation. Hips should be pressed slightly forwards and upwards causing the feet to press backwards and downwards into the bed.

2. The body remains straight after take-off showing only slight rotation then, just before the landing, the relevant position is shown.

3. Land on the cross with legs together and straight and in contact with the bed from heels to hips. Toes should be pointed. Hands are kept flat, just behind and to the side of the hips, with fingers pointing forwards. The trunk should be leaning back a little with the weight slightly on the hands.

USE OF ARMS

The arms are used to jump both into the landing and out of it. Good arm positioning in all the basic moves makes learning subsequent progressions easier.

POSITIVE TERMINOLOGY

The new use of the word 'landing' instead of 'drop' is a reminder that the action is a positive one, with the performer completing the take-off and flight phases before the landing position is shown.

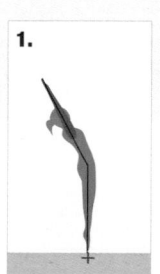 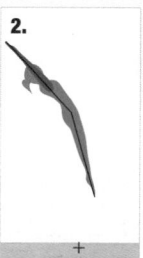 

Seat landing
1. Take-off
2. Flight
3. Landing

HANDS AND KNEES LANDING

1. Take-off with feet pushed backwards and the trunk and arms moving up and forwards.

2. Land with knees and hands simultaneously. Hold a 90-degree angle at the armpits, with back flat, neck straight and facing forward. Keep feet flat on the bed, not with the toes curled under. Return to feet by pushing with hands.

Knee landings are not recommended as it is easy to cause back damage. However, they can be an option to make safe a faulty landing.

FRONT LANDING

1. Take-off with feet pushed backwards and the trunk and arms moving up and forwards.

2. Use a forward somersault rotation to land on the front of the body.

3. Hands, chest, stomach and thighs should land simultaneously, with hips on the cross. Keep the arms in a diamond shape under the chin, with hands just in front of the face on the bed. The forearm and hand should be in contact with the bed. Toes point towards the ceiling. Return to feet by pushing with hands and flipping down feet.

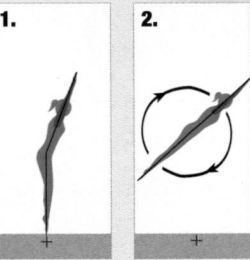

Hands and knees landing
1. Take-off last contact
2. Flight
3. Landing

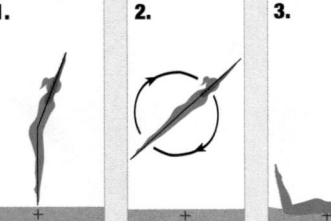

Front landing
1. Take-off last contact
2. Flight
3. Landing

A common mistake when learning the front landing is to lean forward rather than push the feet back and up. This may injure the back. Use a mat to practise.

BACK LANDING

1. Take off with hips forward and up.

2. Flight.

3. On landing, the head must touch the bed at the same time as the back. Hips to head should be flat on the bed. Keep arms and legs vertical and straight. Focus on the ceiling. Return to feet by slightly bending the knees then pushing feet upwards and forward with feet towards the bed.

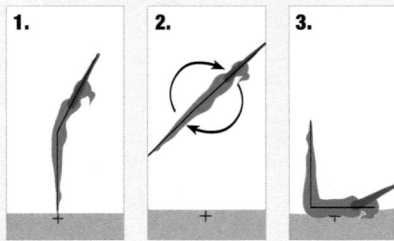

Back landing
1. Take-off last contact
2. Flight
3. Landing

> It is easier to do a half-twist to feet off a back landing rather than come straight up, as it allows for better vision of the bed.

INTRODUCING TWIST

Experimenting with twists to and from different landings enables the gymnast to learn how to speed up and slow down. A long, narrow shape (straight) twists easily but a shorter, wider one (tuck) does less well.

TWISTING JUMPS

The power required for a twist is very small – most gymnasts can do a half- and full-twist on the floor without a trampoline. Preferred twist direction can be determined using a half-twist to feet from front and back landings. All twisting moves should then be taught to turn that way.

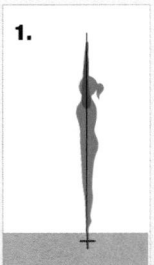
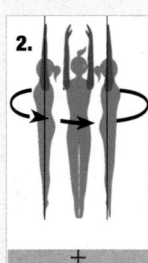
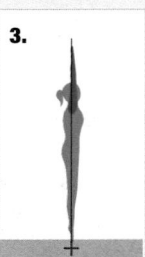

Half-twist jump.

BASIC ROUTINES

ROUTINE A	ROUTINE B	ROUTINE C
1. Front landing	1. Front landing	1. Half-twist jump
2. To feet	2. To feet	2. Straddle jump
3. Straddle jump	3. Straddle jump	3. Seat landing
4. Half-twist jump	4. Half-twist jump	4. Half-twist to seat landing
5. Tuck jump	5. Tuck jump	5. Half-twist to feet
6. Seat landing	6. Seat landing	6. Pike jump
7. Half-twist to seat	7. Half-twist to feet	7. Back landing
8. Half-twist to feet	8. Pike jump	8. Half-twist to feet
9. Pike jump	9. Back landing	9. Tuck jump
10. Full-twist jump	10. Half-twist to feet	10. Full-twist jump

ROUTINES

Trampoline competitions are based on routines where the competitor has to complete ten different skills, after a few introductory bounces, with only one bed contact between each.

Beginners learn linking skills with a straight bounce in between, and then try consecutive shaped jumps. By adding different landing positions and types of twist the choice of moves is wide.

Here are some simple linked skills, which involve twist:

- swivel hips: seat landing, half-twist to seat landing
- roller: seat landing, full-twist to seat landing
- cradle: back landing, half-twist to back landing
- cat twist: back landing, full-twist to back landing.

Apart from swivel hips, these moves are rarely used in routines but are important progressions in the long-term development of the gymnast.

Now the gymnast may enter novice competitions (see pages 40–47).

Erin Blanchard of the USA
performs at the Beijing
Olympics, 2008, in China.

INTERMEDIATE MOVES

When the trampolinist becomes more competent and can perform the basic moves confidently, they may be interested in entering competitions. The next stage is to master the intermediate moves.

MASTERING NEUTRAL POSITION

For the intermediate skills, the body should reach the neutral position both at the beginning of the take-off and at the end of the landing in every move. This ensures that the moves flow more consistently.

LINE OUTS (see page 14)

The diagrams in this chapter show the correct line outs. However, trying to achieve early straight line outs when the quality of somersault is inadequate can be counterproductive and possibly dangerous. Earlier, straighter and longer-held exits develop gradually as a result of long-term practice. Mastering posture and timing during the bed contact period, followed by efficient shape closure in flight is also important.

CONSOLIDATION

Once a skill, combination or sequence has been learned, the trampolinist should practise over time until they feel confident before progressing. Failure to allow this consolidation period may hamper further development and put the trampolinist at risk.

Flat back is the same as the back landing, but with legs flat on the bed. This is a useful move when beginning to combine somersault and twist, as twist can be done late just before contact (see page 33).

THREE-QUARTER TURN OVER

From a foot landing this move rotates forward on to a back landing.

Progression 1: Forward roll

Progression 2 (below): Take-off from hands and knees, keeping the head clear of the bed as the body turns over.

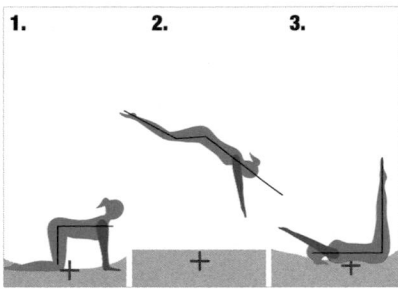

Progression 3: Take off from a crouching stance.

Progression 4 (below): Bouncing upright, take-off with full height lift into the three-quarter turn over. Good vision of the bed can be maintained until the folding into the back landing.

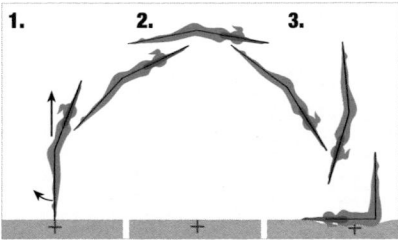

In a back landing from a forward rotation, the arms should be held back in line with the ears during the approach. This minimises the curve in the back that can cause an unstable landing.

BACK PULL OVER

This is the reverse of the three-quarter turn over. It is performed from the back landing when the performer pushes their legs back and up over the head, creating backward rotation.

PROGRESSING TO SOMERSAULTS

The three-quarter turn over and the back pull over are seldom used in competitions. Once a gymnast is competent at a three-quarter turn over, they progress on to a complete front somersault or a three-quarter somersault straight. It is more usual to somersault forward from a back landing.

FRONT SOMERSAULT

Once a trampolinist has mastered the three-quarter turn over, a front somersault can be introduced. This is a 360-degree forward somersault from feet to feet.

The tucked front somersault is the safest one to try first, as the head is tucked under early to minimise risk of serious neck injury. However, the landing is 'blind' as the gymnast cannot see the bed during the landing stage. Maximum support is used for first attempts at somersaults. Support is reduced only when the pupil shows consistent performance, correct technique and confidence.

Further developments

• Pike front somersault

Front somersaults in the straight shape are used as a step towards twisting somersaults. They are rarely performed on their own because of the blind landing.

Front somersault
1. Take-off. A small forward bend with feet pushed backwards and up on last contact gives somersault rotation.
2. Flight. From a straight-legged push, knees are pulled into a tight tuck.
3. Landing. Raise arms before first contact.

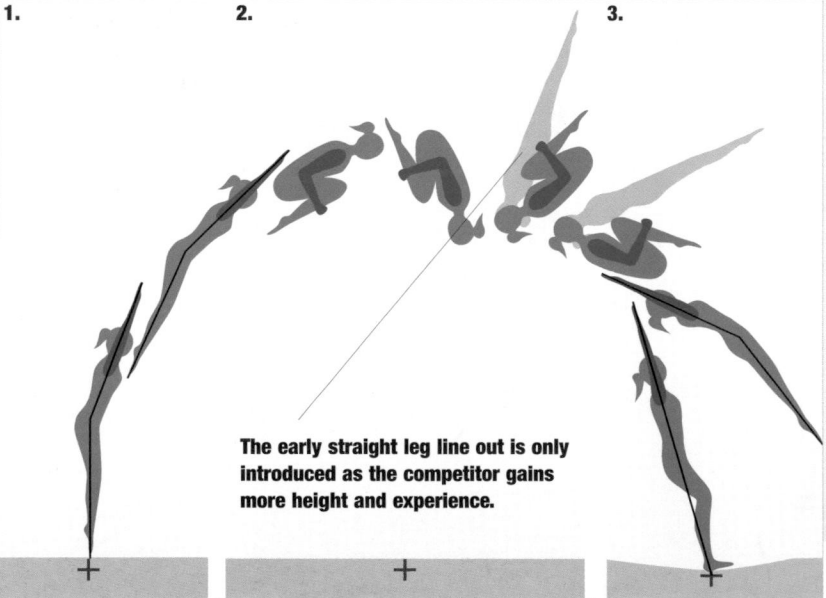

1.   **2.**   **3.**

The early straight leg line out is only introduced as the competitor gains more height and experience.

BACK SOMERSAULT

This is a 360-degree backwards somersault from feet to feet. Often a straight back somersault is taught first. Although it takes more power to somersault the body in the straight shape, it does allow greater vision and the gymnast can tuck into the landing if they are short of rotation.

Further developments

- Tucked back somersault
- Piked back somersault
- Back somersault to seat

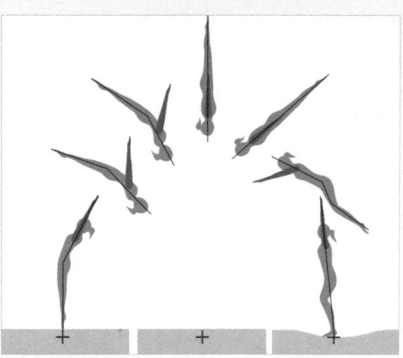

Back somersault
1. Take-off. Push hips forward and up.
2. Flight. Arms are held straight as the body rises to meet them.
3. Landing. Arms rising as bed depresses.

Piked back somersault exit with line out (below)

This is where a straight line should be shown from the shape exit and held until the landing approach. Piked is the most difficult of the back somersault shapes as the hip lift and straight extension on take-off make pulling up into a pike shape difficult. Once the performer can do a good piked back somersault they should be ready to introduce a line out, initially in the easier tucked back somersault.

A good straight back somersault allows for progression into twists.

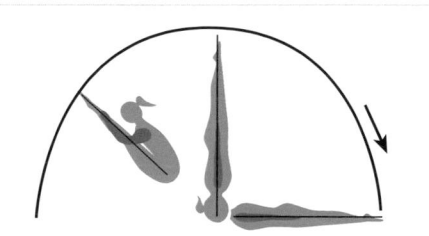

Competition judges look for the straight body shape being held as long as possible before the break in line in preparation for landing.

FRONT SOMERSAULT WITH HALF-TWIST

This somersault is also known as a 'barani'. The somersault rotation at take-off must be fast enough and provide enough height for the trampolinist to form the straight body shape needed to perform the twist. A high pike front somersault that over-rotates is an indication that the gymnast has enough power to progress to learn a barani.

Progressions

- Piked and straight baranis

Adding an extra half-twist makes a full-twisting somersault. This is rarely used in competition because it results in the blind front landing. Adding extra twists to a single front somersault creates increasingly complex competition moves:

- one and a half twists (a rudolph)
- two and a half twists (a randolph)
- three and a half twists (an adolf).

Front somersault with half-twist (tuck)

1. Take-off. A small forward bend combined with feet pushing backwards and up on last contact gives somersault rotation.

2. Flight. From a straight-legged push, move quickly into a high, tight shape (tuck).
3. Twist and line out simultaneously, maintaining good vision of the bed.
4. Landing. Arms rising as bed depresses.

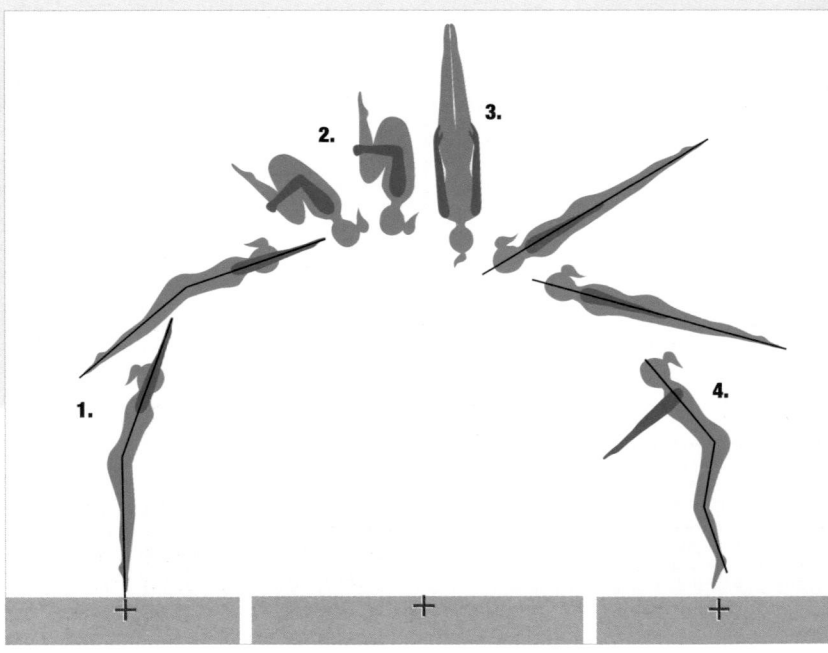

THREE-QUARTER FRONT, STRAIGHT TO BACK

Formerly known as a 'crash dive', the three-quarter front straight is usually taught after the front somersault, as the gymnast needs to be able to hold the straight line on the landing approach.

Prior progression

- A high quarter-somersault rotation into a straight front landing.

Practice drill

1. A three-quarter front, straight to back

2. Half-twist to feet

3. Tuck jump

4. Repeat

KEEP PRACTISING

A tucked front somersault is the easiest to rotate. Adding a twist, thereby converting it to a barani, means the landing is no longer 'blind'. It is quite common for a trampolinist to 'lose' their front somersault once they learn a barani, as they feel more secure seeing the bed throughout. It is best to continue practising ordinary somersaults regularly while learning the barani.

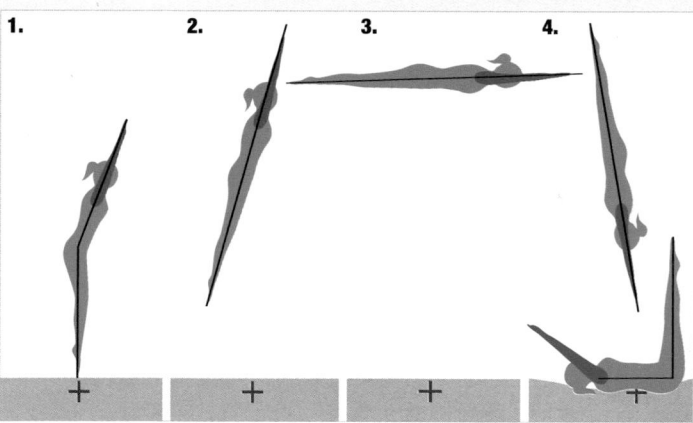

Three-quarter front somersault

1. Take-off. A forward bend on last contact gives somersault rotation.

2. Flight.

3. Landing approach. The whole body should be straight.

4. Landing. Secure back landing with shoulders down, arms by ears and feet high allows for progression to somersaulting off the back landing.

THREE-QUARTER BACK SOMERSAULT TO FRONT

This move was formally known as a 'lazy back', because of the slow somersault rotation in the straight position. It is difficult to limit over-rotation in this move, apart from extending the arms. However, as the gymnast has full view of the bed from the top of the move they can tuck in and land on hands and knees or feet if necessary. The ability to sense errors and correct them safely is an important skill for all trampolinists.

Variations

A tucked or piked three-quarter back somersault are good moves to demonstrate an excellent line out and holding of the straight line into the bed.

Three-quarter back, then one and a quarter back somersault

This move was formally known as a 'lazy back cody'. A high front landing, as given by a three-quarter back somersault provides a high enough rebound to somersault out.

The use of a push-in mat is recommended when learning body landings from new amounts of rotation.

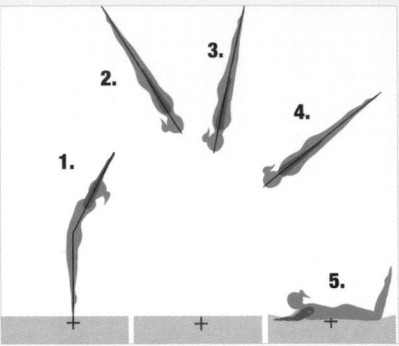

Three-quarter back somersault (lazy back)
1. Take-off
2. Hip lift into take-off
3. Flight
4. Landing approach
5. Landing

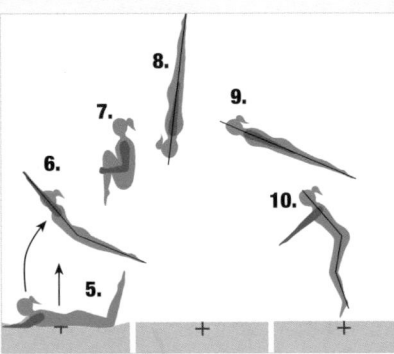

Three-quarter back then one and a quarter back somersault (cody)
1–4. As above
5. Take-off after lazy back
6. Shoulder lift into take-off
7. Flight, fast into tuck
8. Line out
9. Landing approach
10. Landing first contact

CRUISING

Once the trampolinist is comfortable with high front landings, 'cruising' can be introduced. This is a technique used in the flight phase to ease the transition from forward rotation to backwards or vice versa. The simplest form of cruising is the front landing half-twist to front.

This reinforces the concept of the reactive twist, where the competitor keeps the trampoline in sight throughout to learn to accommodate and correct errors. This helps the trampolinist to develop complex twisting multiple somersaults.

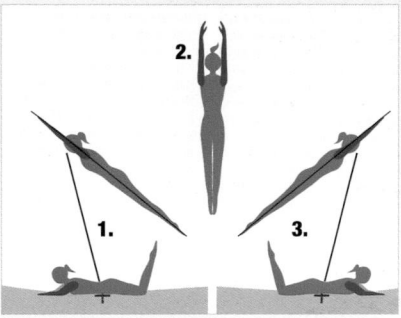

Front half-twist to front landing
1. Back somersault rotation
2. Cruise half-twist
3. Front somersault rotation

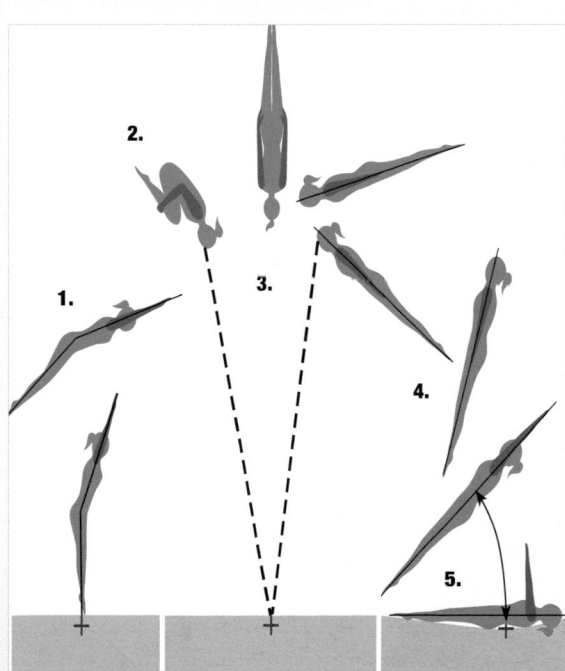

The intermediate bouncer can start experimenting with this technique to combine familiar moves.

Barani to back (front somersault with half-twist to back landing)
1. Take-off last contact
2. Front somersault rotation
3. Cruise half-twist
4. Back rotation
5. Flat back landing

LINKING SOMERSAULTS

The challenge in linking somersaults is that the rotation for each move has to be controlled accurately before the next skill can be performed consistently. When starting to link somersaults the trampolinist must become comfortable with perceived 'short' touchdowns, because the upright position should be at maximum depression of the bed, and not on first contact.

Any rotation set up on take-off needs to be stopped on landing, so the first contact with the bed out of a somersault should be short of the vertical. The objective is to be upright and in the neutral position by the time the bed arrives at full depression.

Ideally the point of exit from every somersault should be identical in order to create a perfect touch down. This creates a consistent and predictable take-off for all follow-on moves.

If one somersault is faulty, a special effort to attain a vertical neutral position during the landing can help save the rest of the routine.

Linking somersaults
1. Front somersault half-twist
2. Neutral position
3. Back somersault

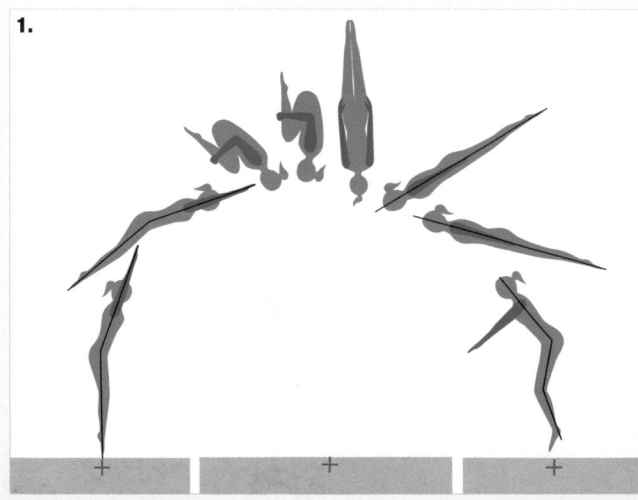

INTERMEDIATE ROUTINES

ROUTINE A

1. Back S/S (S)
2. Barani (S)
3. Piked straddle jump
4. Back S/S (T)
5. Barani (T)
6. Tuck jump
7. Back S/S to seat jump (T)
8. Half-twist to feet
9. Pike jump
10. Front S/S (P)

ROUTINE B

1. Back S/S (S)
2. Barani (S)
3. Back S/S (P)
4. Barani (P)
5. Piked straddle jump
6. Back S/S (T)
7. Barani (T)
8. Back S/S to seat drop (T)
9. Half-twist to feet
10. Front S/S (P)

ROUTINE C

1. Back S/S (S)
2. Barani (S)
3. Full twisting back S/S
4. Piked straddle jump
5. Back S/S (P)
6. Barani (P)
7. Back S/S (T)
8. Three-quarter front somersault (S)
9. Ballout barani (T)
10. Front S/S (P)

KEY

S/S = SOMERSAULT. (P) = PIKED. (S) = STRAIGHT. (T) = TUCKED.

2.

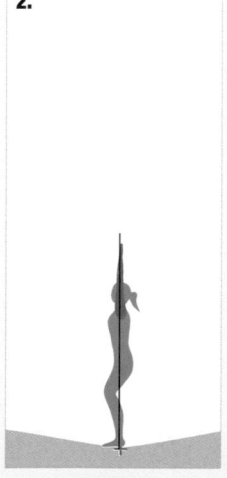

3.

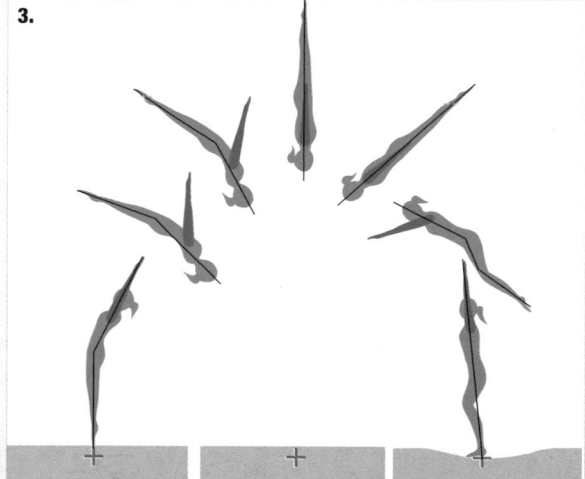

ADVANCED MOVES

All advanced moves are just multiples and combinations of the skills already learned by the trampolinist. As long as the coach has led the trampolinist through the correct progressions, the performer should have the necessary skills, strength, fitness, spatial awareness and experience to work on this level.

> Only higher-level coaches (Senior Club Coach and above) are qualified to teach advanced moves without supervision. They should never be attempted without carefully planned skills progression.

DIFFICULTY SHOULD BE EASY!

With the proper coaching, progression and practise, the gymnast should have naturally developed the skills needed to perform the advanced moves. These moves are awarded increased difficulty bonus points in competitions. The earlier work on take-offs, aerial skills and landings should now really pay off. By combining the same elements in different orders even more variety

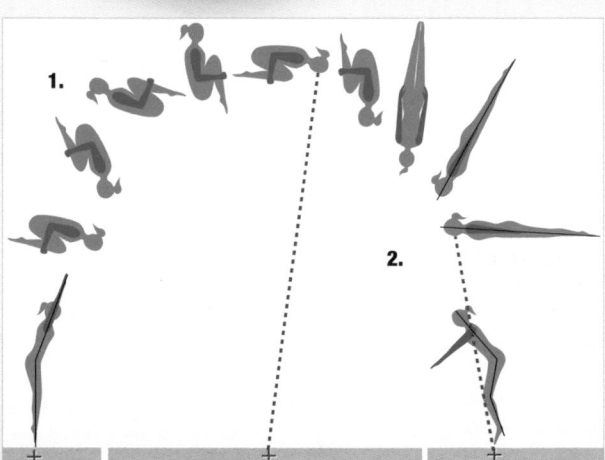

'Half out' or 'barani out' i.e. double forward somersault with a half-twist in the second somersault
The body bend should not appear before the three o'clock angle.

1. Forward somersault
2. Barani (front somersault with a half-twist)

can be produced. For example, a double front somersault with a half-twist can be done in two ways:

- twist in the first somersault (half-in)
- twist in the second somersault (half-out) as shown in the diagram on page 36.

A double back with a full-twist can be done in three ways:

- half-twist in each somersault (half-in half-out)
- all the twist in the first (full-in)
- all the twist in the second (full-out).

These all count as different moves in a competition routine.

DOUBLE AND TRIPLE SOMERSAULTS

Double and even triple somersaults are now becoming commonplace in national level competition. This is thanks to improvements in the equipment, the health and fitness of the competitors and a greater understanding of how trampolining works. However, the number of somersaults is rarely more than three and the number of twists rarely more than four.

Double (or triple) front somersaults are rare because of the blind landing. It is more usual for the performer to 'barani out' so they have clear vision of the bed on landing.

WHEN THE TIME IS RIGHT

A talented gymnast may be tempted to try advanced moves whilst still relatively inexperienced. However, without the correct foundation of techniques, bad habits can form, which may be unsafe and will have to be corrected later, and so can delay the trampolinist's competitive progress.

Even in multiple somersaults the straight body line out should be shown from the shape exit until just before landing.

INTRODUCING TWIST BY CRUISING

Cruising, as discussed on page 33, is considered by some experts to be one of the safest and most productive methods of introducing twist into multiple somersaults. The individual moves are effectively separated by a clear transition (the cruise), which gives clarity for both the performer and the coach, and ultimately can lead to competition success at the highest levels. The diagram below shows how a double back somersault with full-twist (back in full-out) can be constructed. This method gives three visual check opportunities.

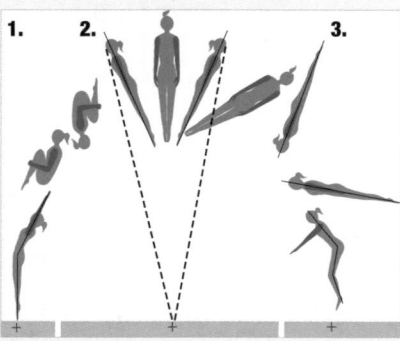

Back in, full-out
1. Back somersault
2. Cruise half-twist
3. Barani (front somersault with a half-twist)
(The dotted lines indicate the trampolinist's line of sight.)

ADVANCED ROUTINES

The possible combinations of somersault, twist and shape are huge. Top-level competitors are not given set routines, just compulsory elements following the international FIG rules. This allows for the demonstration of the very best combinations of moves and is one thing that makes the sport of trampolining so exciting and interesting to watch.

FIG 'B' SET

Ten different elements, nine of them with a minimum of 270-degree somersault and must include:

1. one front or back landing
2. one element from front or back in conjunction with requirement no (1)
3. one double somersault with or without twist
4. one element with a minimum of 540 degrees twist.

Elements cannot be combined to fulfil the above requirements.

FIG 'A' SET

Ten different elements, each with a minimum of 270 degrees rotation, including two elements for which the difficulty score is added.

 The modern arena is far better equipped and safety is of paramount importance.

COMPETITIVE TRAMPOLINING

Competitive trampolining is a relatively new sport as it really only took off in the second half of the twentieth century. Competition began in the USA at the end of the Second World War, spreading to Europe in the 1950s. Display teams took it worldwide in the late 1950s and early 1960s, which is when many national federations were formed.

Visit www.british-gymnastics.org to find the full set of rules governing National Grading competitions.

TRAMPOLINING COMPETITION MILESTONES

- 1957 – first UK Open Trampoline Competition was at a water carnival organised by the Ilford Diving Club. The winner was Mick Forge.

- 1959 – first UK National Trampoline Championships in Stanmore Park, Middlesex.

- 1964 – first World Championships, held in London, UK.

- 1969 – first European Championships.

- 1981 – first Pan Pacific Championship.

- 2000 – trampolining became an Olympic sport.

TYPES OF COMPETITIONS

Regional and national competitions are organised in groups based on age and ability. The complex history of trampolining in Britain means there is a wide variety of competitions available at regional level, not all following British Gymnastics (BG) rules.

INDIVIDUAL TRAMPOLINING NATIONAL GRADING STRUCTURE

The National Grading structure has been developed to support Long Term Athlete Development (LTAD). The grades ensure that the competitor attains a good quality of performance at each level and learns the correct progressive skills before taking part at the next grade.

Serious trampolinists in the UK aim to work their way to the top of the National Grading system to the National Finals, which are held in July each year. Only the top competitors in the country may enter and the winners become the British Champions. Double Mini Trampolining (DMT) and Trampoline competitions are combined and referred to as Gala competitions, which are held over a weekend.

SCHOOLS COMPETITIONS BRITISH SCHOOLS GYMNASTIC ASSOCIATION (BSAG)

Schools competitions are held between November and March. There are two levels of competition to encourage school and club competitors to participate.

REGIONAL COMPETITIONS

Regions organise local competitions such as:

- inter-club competitions
- tariff-based competitions
- regional championships
- inter-regional matches.

International competitions allow improving gymnasts to compete alongside some of the best in the world.

INTERNATIONAL AND OPEN INTERNATIONAL EVENTS

There are a number of Open International Events held abroad each year. Competitions are open to any club with competitors that can complete the compulsory elements.

For the following international events selections are made based upon the National Squad Selection Criteria:

- World Senior Championships
- European Senior Championships
- World Cup Events
- European Youth Championships
- Youth International v Germany: an annual event for over 36 years
- International Age Group Games: A biannual celebration for over 30 years, run in conjunction with the World Championships and well supported by British Trampolining.

UK TRAMPOLINE COMPETITION STRUCTURE

This is designed to be developmental, following the expert recommendations for Long Term Athlete Development (LTAD), from Club I level through to FIG A.

- Learning to Train: acquiring basic skills
  Entry Level: Club I and H events are run either within a club or regionally. The emphasis is on participation and fun whilst developing good technique.

- Training to Train: acquiring key skills
  Performance level: G to E assessments are run regionally four times a year and are the early learning stages for competition, i.e. presenting oneself in public, wearing competition uniform, learning to control nerves, gaining consistency of performance in completing routines and knowing and understanding the competition rules.

- Training to Compete: acquiring advanced skills
  National League: Regional D competitions are run and held within each region and National C and FIGs B and A are run nationally in Gala events.

- Training to Win: refining and maximising skills. FIG A is the highest level of competition within the UK.

ROUTINES

The first routine in National Grading competitions is either a set routine where all 10 moves are dictated, or at the higher levels a 'free' routine in which the competitor has to include a number of compulsory skills, which can be awarded difficulty bonuses.

The second routine (voluntary) and final routines carry a difficulty mark, which is added to the execution marks. It may be tempting to include some big moves in the voluntary routine, even if they are inconsistent. However, form and technique are more important than difficulty and the scoring system underlines this. A 0.3 increase in difficulty can be wiped out by a 0.1 loss in form on a single move.

CONSTRUCTION OF ROUTINES

Simple shaped jumps are useful to prepare for, and space out, moves that the competitor may find more difficult. Any move resulting in a body landing can limit the choice of the next move by restricting the amount of height and rotation the competitor can achieve. When several consecutive somersaults are included in a routine it is usual to alternate backward and forward rotating skills to aid balance and keep the routine flowing.

NATIONAL GRADING COMPETITIONS

The order for National Grading competitions is as follows:

1. Preliminary rounds

- Warm-up (set routine)
- Compete (set routine)
- Warm-up (voluntary routine)
- Compete (voluntary routine)

2. Finals
The eight best scores from preliminary rounds, in reverse order of merit.

- Warm-up (final routine)
- Compete (finals routine)

3. Presentation to winners
The winner is the one with the most points. There are no ties or equal places.

COMPETING TEAMS

A team comprises three or four members of a single club, all wearing the same outfit and competing in the same age group.

As long as a team begins the first round with three competitors, it is valid. Team events score over the first two routines only. The resultant score is made up of the highest three set routine scores and the highest three voluntary routine scores from any three members of the team.

COMPETITION CLOTHING

Although not as formal as tennis or cricket, there are rules about what trampolining competitors should wear. Long hair must be tied back and no jewellery, watches or body piercings may be worn.

Members of a team must wear matching clothing.

- Female leotard (sleeved or sleeveless), white trampoline shoes or ankle socks (trampoline shoes are secure-fitting foot coverings with soft non-slip soles).

- Male sleeveless leotard; light, single coloured trousers; footwear in white or to match trousers.

Spotters and marshals should wear a tracksuit and gym shoes.

Female competition attire.

 Male competition attire.

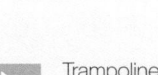 Trampoline shoes.

COMPETITION LAYOUT

The layout of any competition venue is designed to maximise safety and the use of the equipment, people and available space. The competition floor manager has the role of ensuring that the floor area at the competition is kept as clear as possible.

At national level Gala weekends, DMT competitions run at the same time as individual.

WHO'S WHO AT A COMPETITION?

As well as the competitor, there are officials present during competitions. At all National Grading competitions the officials will be as described below, but there may be some variation at local level. When entering a competition every club has to nominate a proportionate number of suitably qualified officials for their competitors. Competitors must have one spotter/un-matted side of the bed for their warm-up, and two/un-matted side during the competition. A competitor can use their own, or the official spotters,

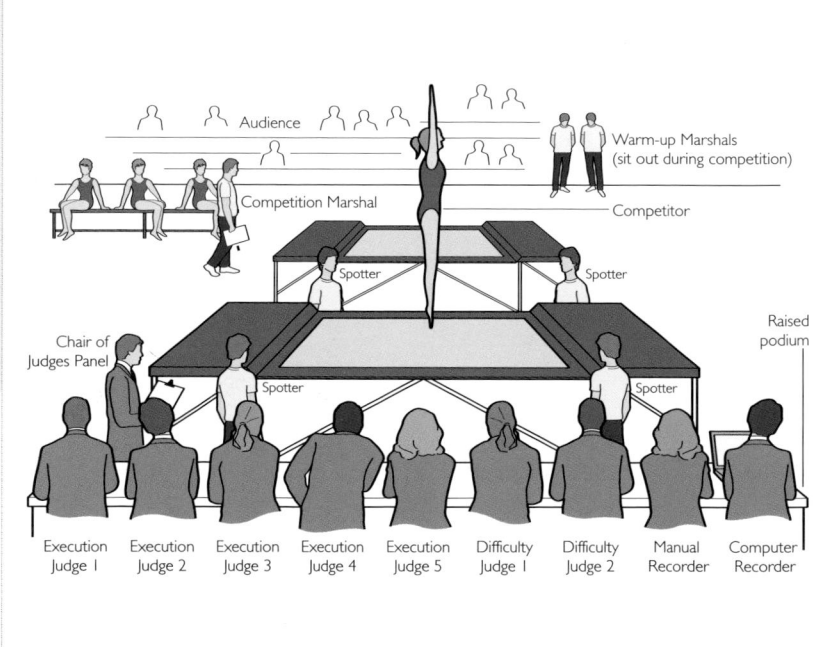

as they choose. There are also two Warm-up Marshals to supervise warm-ups before competing. One Competition Marshal supervises the competitors during the competition. They make sure that the competitors are in the right place at the right time. A Computer Recorder enters scores from the judges on a computer, and prints out the start order and results. A Manual Recorder is there for backup, in case the computer crashes. An independent Welfare Officer is provided for each event.

EXECUTION JUDGING

Execution is how well the routine is performed. It is marked out of a maximum score of 10. There are deductions designed to encourage safety and excellent technique. 0.0–0.5 deductions are made for any performance imperfections. The minimum score for poor form alone is 5.0. Further deductions are also made for contravening competition rules, for example 1.0 for un-sportsmanlike conduct and 0.1–0.3 for a delayed start of a routine.

The Chair of Judges

The Chair of the Judges Panel is in overall charge, dealing with any queries about possible errors in the difficulty scores or any infringement of rules. There are usually five Execution Judges who score how well each element is performed. Marks are deducted for faults. There are also two Difficulty Judges who score the difficulty of each move and ensure the routines are correct.

SCORING

The scores displayed by the Execution Judges are between 0.0 and 10.0. Deductions are made for errors of form, instability, rule contravention and penalties from the total number of moves completed (usually 10). Generally, the Execution Judges look for the following:

- the whole move looks easy and smooth
- hands are in line with the body
- arms are straight, in line
- toes and feet are pointed and together
- legs are together, (apart from straddle) no gaps when twisting
- legs are bent only in the tuck shape
- there is no travel
- the head is in line with the body
- there are three distinct phases (take-off, flight, landing).

Take-off phase:

- there is a straight leg drive into the skill
- there is a delay before the shape.

Flight phase:

- there is consistent height
- there are defined shapes, as tight as possible
- there is twist efficiency
- timing is completed before the final phase
- somersault exits – there is timing, line is held, there is vertical line out.

Landing phase:

- is straight until the bed approach
- there is minimised piking or tucking in.

JUDGING DIFFICULTY (TARIFF)

The Difficulty Judges calculate the total difficulty score (tariff) of the voluntary routines. Marks are awarded based on the number of quarter-somersaults and half-twists, and the shape of the moves. The more twists and rotations, the higher the tariff. Bonus points are given for complete somersaults and more difficult shapes.

THE FINAL SCORE

For each routine the Recorder adds the three middle execution scores, and deletes the highest and lowest. For example:

Execution Judge 1	7.5
Execution Judge 2	~~7.4~~
Execution Judge 3	7.6
Execution Judge 4	7.6
Execution Judge 5	~~7.7~~
Total	**22.7**

Difficulty scores (tariffs) are then added: for example $22.7 + 4.4 = 27.1$

The winner is the one with the most points, with no ties or equal places.

JUDGE AWARDS

Becoming a top level judge takes years of training and only the most qualified judges officiate at Grade 1 competitions. The British Gymnastics trampolining qualifications are as follows:

- British Gymnastics Club Judge Award
- British Gymnastics County Judge Award
- British Gymnastics Regional Judge Award
- British Gymnastics Zonal Judge Award
- British Gymnastics National Judge Award
- British Gymnastics Brevet Judge Award.

A proud winning team display their hard-earned trophy.

ALTERNATIVE TRAMPOLINING

Trampolining in the UK includes two other recognised sub-disciplines: Synchronised and Double Mini Trampolining (DMT). Trampolines are also in use outside the sporting world. The Royal Air Force, and later the Space Agencies, quickly employed trampolines to train their pilots and astronauts. The trampoline also has medical uses in helping people with special needs.

A pair of trampolinists in perfect synchronisation.

SYNCHRONISED TRAMPOLINING

Synchronised Trampolining is similar to Individual Trampolining but is performed by two competitors on separate, full-sized FIG-approved trampolines with webbed beds. In order to be allowed to compete as a pair, at least one performer has to be of the same grade as the competition and the partner must be either of an equal grade or lower. Where competitors are from different age groups they must compete in the age group of the older partner. The pair can be from different clubs. The trampolines must be arranged in matching pairs. At competition level, the pair must perform two (or three) ten-element routines as for Individual Trampolining. Each pair is expected to perform identical ten-move routines simultaneously. The routine is the same for all groups and is 10 different skills, including:

A. seven skills with a minimum of 270 degrees of somersault rotation

B. one skill from (A) must be either a full twisting back somersault, or one twisting front somersault, or one skill landing on either the front or back, and from this skill one skill with a minimum of 450 degrees of somersault rotation.

Qualification for the Synchronised British Championships is by ranking points gained at the Gala weekends. The British Synchronised Trampoline Championships is held alongside the British Trampoline Championships in July.

JUDGING

There are four Execution Judges, two for each bed. They award marks out of 10. The difference in height and timing of the landings of the pair is measured by a de-synchronisation machine or by three judges.

DOUBLE MINI TRAMPOLINING (DMT)

At the elite level, DMT is one of the most spectacular sports, with competitors completing high, multi-twisting somersaults. An elongated version of a 'mini' trampoline is used for DMT competitions, with both ends open and marked by elastic bungees. Red lines outline the safe areas to land: the sloping 'mount' and the flat 'spotter' areas.

> **DMT coaches must be specially qualified; a DMT International Performance Coach is required for double somersaults with more than a double twist.**

A double mini trampoline.

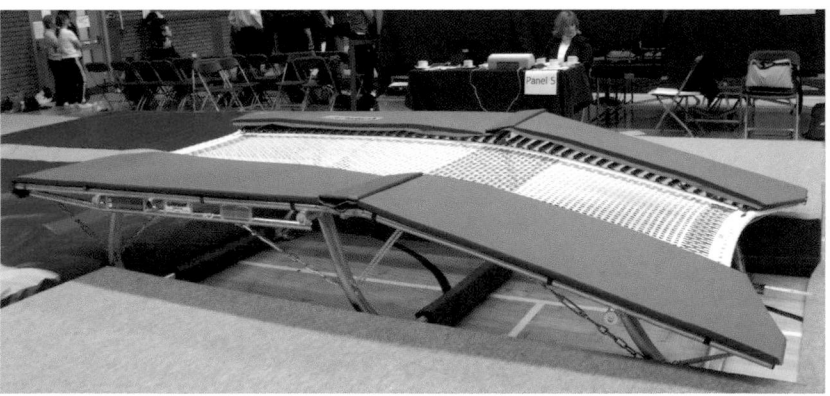

DMT COMPETITION

DMT and Trampoline competitions are combined and referred to as Gala competitions, and are held over whole weekends. A single competitor performs two or four 'passes' on a mini trampoline. Each pass consists of two skills that must start and end on the feet. The first skill is performed on either of the two areas on the apparatus, followed by the dismount on to the landing mat.

There are two preliminary passes then the finalists (a maximum of eight) do two final passes.

Clothing

Girls: Long- or short-sleeved leotards and white socks/white DMT shoes.

Boys: Leotard and gym shorts and white socks/white DMT shoes.

DMT JUDGING

DMT Execution Judges use the same criteria as trampolining, where both elements of each pass are marked for errors (0.0–0.5) and subtracted from a maximum score of 10. DMT Difficulty Judges award much higher tariff bonuses for twist and somersault rotation than for individual trampolining.

Home County/Regional D: Each pass must contain a somersault with difficulty capped at 1.3.

National C: Each skill must be a somersault. Preliminary Round must contain either a Barani Mount or Barani Spotter, with difficulty capped at 2.4.

World FIG B: Each round must contain at least one double somersault.

World FIG A: (Senior Mens and Ladies): each pass must contain a double somersault. Each round must contain a pass with two double somersault skills.

National Finals

• British Double Mini Trampoline Championships: World FIG A

• British Double Mini Trampoline Age Group Competitions: World FIG B

• National C Age Group Finals.

Teams are made up of three or four individuals.

GYMNASTICS AND MOVEMENT FOR PEOPLE WITH DISABILITIES (GMPD)

GMPD was introduced by British Gymnastics to develop and provide training and competitive opportunities for people with any disability recognised by international disability sport organisations. Each competitor competes in two rounds of competition and credit is given to the difficulty of the voluntary round.

The disabilities grades run from GMPD D, with GMPD A as the highest level.

Six skill routines are marked out of 6 plus 4 whole marks to give a mark out of 10.

GMPD D: The voluntary routine is difficulty capped at 0.3.

Set routine: six skills

- no more than ten bounces
- no repeated moves
- correct use of the trampolines' elasticity.

Voluntary routine:

- ten moves/shaped bounces
- no more than twenty bounces

Repeated moves will be allowed, but any repeated move will not be counted when calculating the difficulty mark.

GMPD A: The voluntary routine is difficulty capped at 1.5. Participants may compete either a six contact routine, or a ten contact routine with the following requirements:

Either:

1. Six contact routines to include:

- a twist of no less than 180 degrees
- two of the following, a front, seat or back landing

- participants are permitted one credited repetition of a tariff move
- marks will be out of 6 plus 4 whole marks as per DMT.

Or:

2. Ten contact routines to include:

- a twist of no less than 360 degrees
- a twist of no less than 180 degrees from a seat, front or back landing
- repeats of tariff moves will not be credited
- two rounds of competition with the voluntary round tariffed
- no finals.

Participants with physical or learning difficulties who have the appropriate skill level may compete in the mainstream Grade '7' or above. It should be the aim of both the performer and coach to achieve such a standard as to compete in the higher grades.

GARDEN TRAMPOLINING

Whilst everyone accepts that garden trampolines have great appeal, British Gymnastics has serious concerns regarding the risks involved. British Gymnastics recommends that all trampoline activities should be undertaken in the correct environment under the supervision of British Gymnastics qualified coaches. If you do use a garden trampoline, please follow the safety instructions on the following pages.

BUYING A TRAMPOLINE

Before buying a garden trampoline, you may wish to consider proper training activities for your children in a regulated sports centre environment. If you do decide to buy a trampoline, ensure that you understand all the safety information.

TRAINING

The most important thing is to get proper training on how to use a trampoline. This can be done by attending a club that has British Gymnastics (BG) qualified coaches. The best clubs have GymMark. Watch what's happening and talk to the coaches so you know what is good practice and what to discourage.

SAFETY FIRST

When using a garden trampoline, it is advisable to follow these safety measures:

- Clear the area around the trampoline and do not set the trampoline near trees, fences, poles or other playground equipment.

 Do not allow bouncing followed by jumping off the trampoline.

- Set the trampoline where an energy-absorbing surface (for example, tall grass) surrounds it.
- Use a frame pad that covers the entire area of the spring system.
- Never allow more than one person to use the trampoline at a time.
- If possible, lower the height to ground level by putting the trampoline in a pit.
- Never allow eating or drinking on the trampoline. Chewing gum is particularly dangerous.
- Have someone properly train your child to do stunts and skills.

GARDEN TRAMPOLINE SAFETY RULES

Before using the trampoline, set rules for trampoline safety and discuss them with your child.

- Always supervise children.
- At all times, avoid any skill that involves being upside down, even if the child is trained!
- Remove all jewellery and wear clothing that is not going to catch.
- Do not allow bouncing followed by jumping off the trampoline.
- Have an adequate number of spotters around the edges of the trampoline or netting.

The trampoline netting reduces the risk of injury from a fall.

TRAMPOLINE HALL OF FAME

Although it is still a young sport, trampolining has produced a number of truly talented performers. Here are just a few of them.

DAN MILLMAN (USA)

Millman was the first World Men's Trampoline Champion (1964). He is now a famous author and speaker. His many books, including *Way of the Peaceful Warrior* and *Everyday Enlightenment: The 12 Gateways to Personal Growth*, have been read by millions throughout the world. Millman stays active on his backyard trampoline.

JUDY WILLS CLINE (USA)

Cline was the first World Women's Trampoline Champion (1964). She is in the *Guinness Book of World Records* for holding the most world titles (ten in trampoline, synchronised trampoline and tumbling) and for many years held the record for the most individual titles (with five titles).

Judy Wills Cline now lives with her family and coaches in Las Vegas, USA. She is presently the USA Gymnastics Trampoline and Tumbling National Coach.

ALEXANDER MOSKALENKO (RUSSIA)

Also known as the 'King of Trampoline', Moskalenko is in the *Guinness Book of World Records* as a stand-out performer and one of the best athletes in the world. His major achievements include:

- first ever Olympic Gold medal in trampoline (Sydney, 2000)
- Olympic Silver medal (Athens, 2004)
- World Champion in individual and synchronised trampolining in 1990, 1992, 1994, 1999 and 2001
- World Championship team: 1990, 1992, 1998, 1999, and 2001
- World Championship Silver (individual and team) 2003
- winner of many World Cups.

He has been Head of the Krasnodar Krai Department of Sport since November 2004.

IRINA KARAVAEVA (RUSSIA)

Karavaeva is arguably the best female trampolinist ever. Her many achievements include:

- first ever Olympic Gold medal in trampoline (Sydney, 2000)
- World Champion 1994, 1998, and 1999, 2005
- in 2001, after officially winning a fourth individual World Champion title, she turned her Gold medal over to Anna Dogonadze (Germany) after learning that the difficulty judges had made a mistake
- European Champion 1995, 2000 and 2004
- World Cup Champion 1997, 1999, 2000, 2002 and 2004.

Overall, she won nineteen World Cup competitions. No other female trampolinist won more than six.

PAUL LUXON (GREAT BRITAIN)

Paul became the first European to win the World Champion title in 1972 in Stuttgart, ending the dominance of American trampolinists. The same year, he became World Synchronised Champion with his partner Bob Hughes. Paul also won the European Championships in 1969 and 1971. Amongst many other historic achievements (including becoming the first-ever European Men's Champion in Paris in 1968, and repeating this win in 1971) he became a coach and founded the highly respected and successful Kingston Kites Trampoline Club in Milton Keynes, UK.

INDIVIDUAL TRAMPOLINE WORLD CHAMPIONS FROM THE UK

Paul Luxon 1972
Stewart Matthews 1980
Carl Furrer 1982
Susan Shotton (nee Challis) 1984

BRITISH COMPETITORS IN THE OLYMPIC GAMES INDIVIDUAL TRAMPOLINE

2000 – Lee Brearley, Jaime Moore
2004 – Gary Smith, Kirsten Lawton
2008 – Claire Wright

FAMOUS MOVES

Some trampoline moves have been named after the competitor who first performed them.

Barani
This is a front somersault with a half-twist in any shape. The move was named after Italian circus acrobat and tumbler Alfonso Baroni, who performed it around 1881.

Cody
From front, one and a quarter back somersault in any shape. This move was named after Joe Kotys of Akron, Ohio, USA, one of the few people to compete internationally in both trampoline and gymnastics.

Miller
A triple-twisting double back somersault in any shape. This move was originally performed as two-and-a-half-in, half-out, nowadays usually performed as full-in, double-full-out, with one twist in the first somersault and two twists in the second. It was named after Wayne Miller (USA), winner of the 1966 and 1970 World Championships.

Poliarush
Also known as a Miller Plus or Killer, this double-back somersault with four complete twists in any shape was named after Dimitri Poliarush (BLR), winner of the 1996 World Championships.

Rudolph (rudy)
A front somersault with one and a half twists in any shape. This move was named after Dave Roudolph who executed the move on a trampoline in the late 1920s in vaudeville. Other trampoline moves have been given names that describe the action involved.

Lazy back
A slow, three-quarter back somersault in any shape.

Crash dive
A straight, three-quarter front turnover with a late duck under to back.

Layout back
A straight back somersault.

Swivel hips
Seat landing half-twist to seat landing.

INDIVIDUAL TRAMPOLINE CHAMPIONS

The Olympic Games are held every four years.

Year	Country	Women	Men
2008	China	He Wenna, China	Lu Chunlong, China
2004	Greece	Anna Dogonadze, Georgia	Yuri Nikitin, Ukraine
2000	Australia	Irina Karavaeva, Russia	Alexander Moskalenko, Russia

INDIVIDUAL TRAMPOLINE WORLD CHAMPIONS

The World Championships are now held every two years.

Year	Country	Women	Men
2007	Canada	Irana Karavaeva, Russia	Shuai Yi, China
2005	Netherlands	Irina Karavaeva, Russia	Alexander Rusakov, Russia
2003	Germany	Karen Cockburn, Canada	Henrik Stehlk, Germany
2001	Denmark	Anna Dogonadze, Georgia	Alexander Moskalenko, Russia
1999	South Africa	Irina Karavaeva, Russia	Alexander Moskalenko, Russia
1998	Australia	Irina Karavaeva, Russia	German Khnychev, Russia
1996	Canada	Tatiana Kovaleva, Russia	Dmitri Poliarush, Belarus
1994	Portugal	Irina Karavaeva, Russia	Alexander Moskalenko, Russia
1992	NZ	Elena Merkulova, Russia	Alexander Moskalenko, Russia
1990	Germany	Elena Merkulova, USSR	Alexander Moskalenko, USSR
1988	USA	Rusudan Khoperia, USSR	Vadim Krasnochapka, USSR
1986	France	Tatiana Lushina, USSR	Lionel Pioline, France
1984	Japan	Susan Shotton, UK	Lionel Pioline, France
1982	USA	Ruth Keller, Switzerland	Carl Furrer , UK
1980	Switzerland	Ruth Keller, Switzerland	Stewart Matthews, UK
1978	Australia	Tatiana Anisimova, USSR	Evgeni Janes, USSR
1976	USA	Svetlana Levina, USSR	Evgeni Janes, USSR
1974	South Africa	Alexandra Nicholson, USA	Richard Tison, France
1972	Germany	Alexandra Nicholson, USA	Paul Luxon, UK
1970	Switzerland	Renée Ransom, USA	Wayne Miller, USA
1968	Netherlands	Judy Wills Cline, USA	David Jacobs, USA
1967	UK	Judy Wills Cline, USA	David Jacobs, USA
1966	USA	Judy Wills Cline, USA	Wayne Miller, USA
1965	UK	Judy Wills Cline, USA	Gary Erwin, USA
1964	UK	Judy Wills Cline, USA	Danny Millman, USA

GLOSSARY

Add-on (add-before or add-between) trampoline game Every player has to repeat all the skills of those that went before in the correct order and add a further skill at the end.

Baby fliffus A back landing, half-twist into one and a quarter back somersault.

Back pull over From back, three-quarter back somersault to feet.

Back somersault A 360-degree backward rotation, feet to feet.

Ball out From back, one and a quarter front somersault.

Ball out/Barani From back, one and a quarter front somersault with a late half-twist.

Barani A front somersault with a half-twist.

Bed The sprung part of a trampoline on which trampolinists jump.

Bounce-roll From back, followed by a front somersault, landing again on the back.

Box The outlined rectangular area on a trampoline bed.

British Gymnastics (BG) The national governing body for all British gymnastic disciplines, including trampolining.

British Schools Gymnastic Association (BSGA) The organising body for all British gymnastic disciplines, including trampolining, within schools.

Cast Movement towards either long side of the trampoline frame during a move.

Cat twist From back, followed by one full twist, landing again on the back.

Cody From front, one and a quarter back somersault.

Corkscrew A back landing, half-front somersault with one and a half twists to back.

Cradle From back, half-front somersault with a half-twist to back.

Crash dive A straight three-quarter front somersault.

Degree of Difficulty (tariff) A rating that measures the difficulty of specific moves and is added to the total score after judges have scored the execution of the moves except in set routines.

Double back A 720-degree back somersault rotation without twist.

Double full A single back somersault with two complete twists.

End deck A large, thick mat that sits on a frame at each end of the trampoline to cushion the impact if anyone falls from the apparatus.

Execution 1 The performance of a routine.

Execution 2 The form, style and technique used to complete the skills included in a routine.

Fédération Internationale de Gymnastique (FIG) The organising body for all international gymnastic disciplines, including trampolining. Based in Switzerland.

First contact The finite point at which the first part of the body touches the bed after flight – usually the foot.

Fliffus/Fliff Any double somersault combined with a component of twist.

Forward turnover A three-quarter front somersault, starting from feet. A specific variant in the straight position is termed a 'crash dive'.

Frame The major metal parts of the trampoline.

Front somersault A 360-degree forward rotation from feet to feet.

Full A full-twisting back somersault.

Full-twist jump A 360-degree rotation around the body's twist axis with no somersault.

Gain Travel arising from excessive displacement of the hips in the initiation of somersault movements, for example travelling forwards in a back somersault.

GMPD Gymnastics and Movement for People with Disabilities.

Half-twist jump A 180-degree rotation around the body's twist axis with no somersault.

Jump Positive upwards movement from the feet, harnessing the elasticity of the bed.

Last contact The finite point at which the last part of the body leaves the bed after flight – usually the toes.

Lazy back A three-quarter back somersault.

Line out (kick out) The extension to straight legs and body position after the shape phase of a move.

GLOSSARY

Long Term Athlete Development (LTAD) Introduced by Istvan Balyi in 1990, this is a model that aims to give the most productive and healthiest route for progress through sport training as an athlete matures.

Overhead rig An overhead apparatus with a belt, ropes, pulleys and fittings allowing the coach to provide support for a move whilst learning.

Pass The combination of moves that a competitor performs at any one time on the DMT that is given a single set of scores by the judges. Each pass consists of two skills that must start and end on the feet.

Pike An aerial position where the body is bent forward at the hips at less than 135 degrees or more while the legs are kept straight, with the thighs close to the upper body.

Pike jump A move showing the 'piked' shape, with no rotation or twist.

Press and go The act of pressing with the feet into the bed to give enough height to perform a single skill. Used when learning a new skill when the height gained from taking bounces before it might make it unsafe.

Push-in mat (crash, throw-in or spotter mat) A foam-filled mat used to reduce the rebound when developing a new move. Push-in mat is the preferred term, as it implies a positive, controlled action.

Randolph (randy) A front somersault with two and a half twists.

Rob Roy A back landing, half-front somersault with two and a half twists to back.

Roller A seat landing, full twist to seat.

Routine A series of trampoline skills (usually 10) performed one after the other with no straight jumps in between.

Rudolph (rudy) A front somersault with one and a half twists.

Set (compulsory) A pre-designed routine that contains specific skills and moves.

Somersault (salto) An acrobatic movement where the body makes a complete revolution, heels over head.

Somersault axis The axis roughly defined as through the hips, around which front and back somersaults are done.

Spotter A person who stands at the side of the trampoline and where possible helps to prevent a falling or tripping bouncer hurting themselves.

Spotter mat A small mat which can be thrown on to the bed to help prevent injury. Often used when learning a new move.

Straddle An aerial position where the legs are split at least shoulder width apart and remain straight whilst the upper body is aligned forward at the hips at an angle smaller than 135 degrees.

Straddled jump A move showing the 'straddle' shape, with no rotation or twist.

Straight A position where the body is extended in a straight line, technically defined as the upper body, and the legs are positioned at an angle of more than 135 degrees.

Swivel hips A move starting on the seat, with a half-twist in upright position, then landing again on seat.

Three-quarter turnover (forward turnover) A three-quarter front somersault from feet. A specific variant in the straight position is termed a 'crash dive'.

Travel 1 Movement away from the centre of the bed, with appropriate form deduction.

Travel 2 Movement along the bed in the same direction as the shoulders in a somersault rotation, for example travelling backwards in a back somersault.

Triffus (Triff) Any triple somersault combined with a component of twist.

Tuck An aerial position where the knees are bent and drawn into the chest, with the upper body folded at the waist at an angle less than 135 degrees from the upper legs.

Tucked jump A move showing the 'tuck' shape, with no rotation or twist.

Twist A rotation around the body's twist axis, roughly defined by the spine.

Twist axis The axis from the head through the body, around which twisting is done.

INDEX